MW00791998

HIGH WIND WARNING

High Wind Warning

poems

River Stingray

Casa Urraca Press

ABIQUIÚ

Set in Filosofia and Look Script.

Author photograph by Tyler Griffin.

27 26 25 24   1 2 3 4 5 6 7

First edition

ISBN 978-1-956375-18-3

CASA URRACA PRESS

an imprint of Casa Urraca, Ltd.
PO Box 1119
Abiquiú, New Mexico 87510
casaurracapress.com

For Ty,
for showing me what real love is after all this

Contents

3   Fourteeners

4   Nights on Alameda

5   Sanity

6   Moonlight

7   Pine·cone

8   Bukowski

9   You eon

10   Orion

11   Sourdough

12   Wild·fire

13   Campfire

14   Overlanding

15   Hinge

16   Peanut butter

17   Geronimo

18   Nocturnal

19   Four Seasons

20 Hold me hurt me
21 Taco bell
22 Santa Fe
23 Hungry
24 To go
25 Cowboy
26 Walgreens
27 Chaos
28 Paint
30 Stephen
31 Hell
32 Where do I go?
33 Bandit
34 Black and blue
35 Dreams
36 Without him
37 Assault

38 Bronco

39 Human

40 Ritual (for him)

41 Family

42 Rubicon

43 Cormac

44 Tattoo

45 Coffee

46 Disorient

47 Reckless

48 Forget me not

49 Trailhead

50 Wildflowers

53 Acknowledgments

55 About the author

For so long I've had my eyes
on trails that went one direction
until they grated against sunrises
raging in western skies. I loved
the feeling of unbuttoned days
existing on peaks of granite
exposed, things
no one else saw. So how did I
ever find myself in wet arroyos
running out of wild cactus groves
smiling at the flatness of it all?

Nowhere else can you find
inspiration like this,
going home in your bare feet,
high heels in your dirty hand and you
taste like ramen and apples without
someone noticing you exist

or you're desperate for a hug, as if you were
nine and not lost in your late twenties.

Artists are supposed to live
like this, since you can't say anything
about falling asleep early
most nights. I'd rather be abandoned
elbows-deep at the bar, not bored
during the last leg of a fire
after the kiva is already cold.

Sundays I wander the río
after breakfast, wearing black, almost
naked from the neck up
if no one is watching and I can
take off the expression you liked
yesterday at the empanada café.

Moonlight

Maybe there used to be silver
or something similar suspended
over the saguaros
no one knew about. Anything
lost and I have to find it
in the buried dead of night with campers
going back to their double yellow lines
hoping to sleep while I don't
think they know what they're missing.

Pop-Tarts taste tragic
if you're not waking up in conifers, solo,
nomadic, missing a place you've never been
except in your dreams maybe.

Bukowski

But how did he make loneliness
understand he wasn't the enemy ... he was
kayaking through loose-change emotions
overwhelming anyone like me
who wanted rough hands and
some semblance of a friend
knocking at the door at seven saying
imagine what we could do

Yesterday I ate
only half a burrito
under Orion.

Orion

Outside there are bruised streets
running perpendicular to the taco trucks
in the ribcage of adobe architecture
only Roark could hate. The city
never seems to stay awake.

Sourdough

Sometimes I think I want to
order sourdough pancakes
until I remember he's nine hundred miles away
reading wildlife guides that are no good
down here, in the dark
oven that dries out all the wet roads
under my all-terrain tires. I can't
go over and order us the chai
he used to drink when his girlfriend was gone.

Wild fire

Well, I saw a Mexican gray wolf
inside the tiled kitchen, the cacti
loud against the crispy fur
dwarfing his hungry face.

Can I take you somewhere
around here, where the air
meets the sleeping sugar
pines, turning cold and starry,
for just one night? We should stay up
imagining how tomorrow can be
rescued from the sticky but separate life
each of us is chasing.

Overlanding

Other places don't compare to this
vast sandstone, where your wild eyes will be
echoing between back roads
remote enough to love restlessly
like I love falling asleep on top of cars
and frying pancakes on a propane stove. I want
nothing more than you
dreaming about nylon, undressed
in pale lakes. There are dispersed sites
north where I want to show you how to
go and fall

       off

          the

             map.

How can you decide
if someone is worth sunrise hikes
naked and heavy breakfasts
getting drunk off homemade palomas
even if you work tomorrow?

Peanut butter

Pretty sure you can climb
even with sticky fingers. I've built you
anchors in your favorite sandstone spot
no one else will know about
unless we keep sitting here
three hours into that horizon blur.

Geronimo

Great things happen with a bellyache
evening like this, where everyone
ropes together, hoping plates
on the bar will break harder than their hearts
now that he's pouring his sweet self
into their colored drinks. I go
most nights, watching the pieces picked up
off the coffee-flavored floor.

Nocturnal

Nowhere feels closer than you do
on the champagne-colored road
curving into cerrillos that have gone dark
too quickly. I lose track of time
usually, the coffee gets cold
regardless … every sad song feels good
now that the sunset's drained
and it's just the radio and some snacks and you
left to make it feel right.

Funny how our eyes dripped
over those blonde hills to catch the sunset's
unraveling, our colored drinks
rimmed with isotopic words.

Somehow what I was thinking
escaped you
after another round of cosmos and cranberries
so soft that the cold wasn't cold
outside … maybe I was
never supposed to say what I wanted,
so it wouldn't be silent if you never responded.

Hold me hurt me

Have you ever heard the myth
of a moon man who reminds me of you
looking to love a desert-stained writer
despite knowing he'll get bored of it

maybe by tomorrow. It's just a dream
except he'll never be the same.

Tomorrow the air will be spiced
after this rampant night of naked rain
covering the cars. My hands
overwhelm me when they're alone,

but you bought burritos to fill
empty space inside my painted fingers
like that could do the trick. Maybe
losing you won't be so hard.

Santa Fe

Sometimes the sound of coffee makes me think
about that time we went fishing on the way to
    Ghost Ranch ...
native rainbows hid from your dry eyes
thinking they could escape the draw of your dimples
and all I wanted was something warm in my hands.

Forget that I cried in the car because it was dark,
enamored with ideas of roasted beans in the
    blackened hills.

Hungry

He ordered for the oak table
ugly quesadillas with bruises and beans
nine dollars overpriced ... for a Wednesday
god really let us down
repeatedly. I had nothing to say but
yes, thank you, I don't need anything else.

To go

This stopped being fun, accidentally
overdosing on your late-night words, but

good thing you live in Albuquerque, where I don't
order anything to stick around.

Canyon Road can be lonely
on papery mornings when he's gone
way up north, looking for tortilla chips
because they're warm and make me think
of the times he showed up
yawning, hungrier than I was.

Walgreens

Why would anyone come here
after pouring sours for sleepy
locals with too much to give the bar
gods like himself. He could take whatever
road he wanted home,
early morning money
emptying onto his seat. I was
never someone who would question him
spending time alone, except there.

Can you believe all the things
he told you about hiking and climbing and being
angry at anyone who isn't
only there to watch him make dessert drinks
sweeter than he could ever make himself?

Paint

Pour me down the drain with your tequila
and tell me why you've got to be that guy
in my favorite color eyes saying you're an artist
no one has heard of, your greatest creation
the irresistible expression on your

two fucking faces.

Stephen

Should I stick around
to see if your dark hair vanishes
ever into the wild adobe, stealing
poems you never told me but told me
hurt like hell to write because
everything tasted like tequila
no one was drinking but you.

Hell

He was someone who could brand
every chest with the words he spoke
like a cowboy who never tried
loving things that were wild.

Where do I go?

Why doesn't anyone know
he was my home? He was
east-facing and warm in the winter
rain, pounding into the red dirt
even when the chama wind blew hard

during nights on Canyon Road where
one of us was barefoot.

It's impossible to be there now,

giving out the same smiles
or buying the same color wine.

But why do I only want him
after I'm sad, filling the bathtub with tears
no one thinks exist in the New Mexico
desert — why would you wait for someone
imaginary like him, his poker face
the canvas for things I tried to love.

Black and blue

But I didn't bruise
like you thought I did … I didn't
ache or change
colors like the Santa Fe vista
knocked over on its side

against the horizon, I made art
no one noticed
during the dark sky calls you gave

because your carsick conversations
left more of a permanent mark
under my thin skin. I wish
every word could taste like sips of that.

Dreams

Do you ever think about me
running down a New Mexican highway
except I'm barefoot and brunette
and sticking my thumb out at strangers but
maybe ignoring them all – would you
send someone to pick me up?

Without him

When Sundays seem to last
indefinitely, I know he's gone
to some north-tasting town
he wants to replace the scarred cerrillos
or sad cantinas with … the idea of vanishing
under cowboy blankets in truck beds
tricks me into thinking that I can

have that to myself, if only
in those sleepless dreams I've had
mess with my caffeinated head.

Assault

Another night filled with cherry red
sips out of chilled glasses, with sunset
screaming through the windows
across the warm wash. It's a place
unable to save the person who
loves it … more than anything
the wild dreams hurt the most.

Bronco

But he wasn't supposed to be here
running late and sunbaked stop signs
on the Old Santa Fe Trail, those acetone eyes
never looking at the road or admitting he didn't
care about the way I used to wait around
on this same concrete corner where he would
    speed by.

How does anyone stomach sunset
unless they're three sours in and
maybe don't even notice they are
about to lose sight of a world
nomadic and already gone.

Ritual (for him)

Remember when you were waterproof
in the desert, dry eyes too
tired to soak in any color
unless it came from far enough west, an ambush
after dark watering down the confetti
left in your unbuttered dream.

Fires have been painting New Mexico
and I don't have anyone
making citrus pancakes or arguing
in the smoke-soaked cerrillos, my casita
locked and spiced with cold coffee I made
yesterday, forgotten.

Rubicon

Right now I need something
unrelated to this road, because what
backwards canyon has art galleries
in every visible place, the spicy smell
chiles make, potholes ...
or I guess they all have potholes, but
not ones that can ever be fixed.

Cormac

Can you ever love someone
oblivious to your face and
reckoning with deserts you don't
miss, someone who doesn't know
about how in dreams you name yourself after
canyons they created …

Tattoo

Think I'm addicted to feeling
anything other than broken and brain freezes,
taking long sips of black coffee where
the taste stains my tongue like my ink
obsession, with the desert moon reaching
over the blue bandages I wear.

Creatures of habit don't live here anymore …
only the wild and wasted ones
flexing their sleepy eyes and caffeine
flushing their faithless faces, and you know
escape tastes sweeter than vanilla flavoring
     or feeling
emotions that were never yours.

Disorient

Did anyone notice how
insatiable the New Mexican desert is
since the sun set and the turquoise doors fell
open, my hungry hands
reaching for wine glasses or martini stems
instead of something chewable,
especially filling, the beaded stars
not what I thought they were when I slept
tight with a full stomach.

Restaurants were my favorite place to go
eat food I didn't need and drink
coffee in every cocktail I ordered,
killing time with poetry books that blurred
late-night visions of lonely faces
every time I looked down. There's something
sweet about being barefoot after that
southwest last call.

Forget me not

Fucking up is my sunset habit
or I wouldn't be able to stay awake
remembering his faces and picking scabs
ghosts stuck to my skin in other geographies
even though I feel like I've always lived
the whole time in adobe,

maps for fingers and addictions
eating away at the places I imagined

never leaving. Without you
odds are I'll be gone tomorrow,
trading warm cerrillos for Colorado.

Tuesday I'll be driving north on roads
ruined by April fires, cookie-cutter ponderosas
and bare-breasted sage turning into granite
in a matter of hours. The sun sets,
lattes get cold and I miss the burn
hiking. I feel like I'm fighting
exhaustion in the rearview mirror
and I start searching for something
dreamy to keep me up.

Wildflowers

Why doesn't it look the same
in the high alpine valleys, candy wrappers
lost in the granite scree and banana peels
drying, my eyes
familiar with none of the footprints
lying around and refusing to leave
or to pack out more than just forget-me-nots
with them. I don't want to feel
empty, like the rolling desert
ruined by crowds that I had to abandon
since it felt just like this.

Acknowledgments

From the very beginning, Joanna Stingray, Teresa Zubel, David Levine, and Joan and Fred Nicholas inspired and supported me as a poet. I owe almost all of it to them. The rest I owe to Zach Hively, who seemed to materialize when I needed him the most, and Casa Urraca Press for trusting me to be part of their unbelievable chorus of voices.

River Stingray is drawn to the edges of everything—geography, society, and consciousness—in pursuit of human connection. She has traveled extensively, yet nowhere feels more like her home than New Mexico, where she wrote these poems outside and barefoot. She holds a master's degree in archaeology from the University of Cambridge, and she and her dog, Koa, live in the American West.

Casa Urraca Press publishes creative works by authors we believe in. New Mexico and the U.S. Southwest are rich in creative and literary talent, and the rest of the world deserves to experience our perspectives. So we champion books that belong in the conversation—books with the power, compassion, and variety to bring very different people closer together.

We are proudly centered in the high desert somewhere near Abiquiú, New Mexico. Visit us at casaurracapress.com to browse our books and to register for workshops with our authors.